A VIEW OF
BRITISH POLITICS

KEN ROSS

Copyright@ Ken Ross 2019

I answer a knock on the door to be greeted by political canvassers pleading for votes in the December 12th General Election. They are young, enthusiastic, see success as an agreement with their viewpoint; they are blinded by their masters and unconsciously confused because they have barely licked the realities of life. Rehearsed phrases spill from their lips, framed by smiles that brave the cold winter air. 'Can we rely on your vote?' says a young woman who's perhaps strayed willingly from Leeds University campus.

'The Conservatives will win by a landslide,' I say. 'You're fighting a lost cause.'

'Do you want five more years of austerity?' she says.

'You're still young, it's not your fault, there's so much you have to learn,' I reply.

The other young woman asks if I believe in the current Prime Ministers' lies. She tells me that the National Health Service is about to be sold to the Americans and soon our supermarket shelves will be swollen with chlorinated chicken and that I'll have to sell my house if I get dementia – she's obviously noticed I've passed retirement age and my future looks dire. 'A majority of at least 70,' I say. 'I shall not be voting for Jeremy Corbyn.'

They retreat, I shake my head and feel sympathy; they are trying to knock down a solid wall of revulsion with a feather duster. When parliamentarians attempt to thwart the will of the electorate, they choose the dole queue instead of removing the cotton wool from their eardrums and listening to the people.

Brexit divided this nation not because the populace wished for divisions in society to fester but because the parliamentarians gave voters the freedom to chart a course to their future. A referendum tosses power to the people, and when the result is tossed back to parliament it should not be manipulated or molded into an unrecognizable form. Condescendingly, a majority of parliamentarians claimed that the Leavers did not vote for leaving this way or that way, and the Remainers had education on their side; the unintelligent voice of independence should be crushed by the liberal elitists who simply know better. It mattered not that they tossed power to the ignorant – the ignorant voted foolishly and they must be corrected.

Yes, early December 2019 and Democracy lay perilously wounded on the green seats of the House of Commons. Should Democracy die a quiet death what grim hideous creature shall rise from its corpse? But the voting public was seething unbeknown to the Liberals and a majority of Labour MPs; the incarcerated soul of Democracy was eagerly being willed to die and plans were afoot to bury it where Guy Fawkes placed his gunpowder some four centuries previously. The bowels of the Palace of Westminster seem a good place to bury Democracy.

As during the past thousand days, my viewing of Sky News is unabated. The presenters pick over the intricacies of political comments, political maneuvering, and the words coming from challengers for power. I am no more than millions of other silent assassins awaiting the opening of the poll in several days hence. The parliamentarians who have defied us, those noisy protesters who annoy us, and those who threaten our long-proven method of administration are doomed to failure because they spit in our faces and label us fools.

Even political journalists and folk who should know better after digesting the result of the 2016 referendum are claiming there is a likelihood of a Hung Parliament or a small Conservative majority. The filthy oxygen inside the Westminster Bubble is pickling their brains and the quiet masses beyond London are not in their thoughts. 'Here this,' I say loudly, 'we are primarily Democrats and our silver bullets in the form of voting slips will be fired from barrels of Leavers and Remainers.'

A parliament that is corrupted by its own sense of superiority shall be slain by the wrath of those who first assembled it.

All around me, in houses once owned by Leeds City Council, the busy mothers, decent and wayward fathers, children old enough to think, and senior citizens who've witnessed a plethora of social changes, allow political thinking to temporarily infest their thinking. They have experienced the dithering and the lies and the ridiculous arguments that insult their intelligence; they have undergone an exceptional period in which their democratic voices have been strangled by the bleating wails of those who wish to ignore the peoples' will.

All around me neighbors are revolted by the sick chimes they hear on news bulletins, and not because they deny a right of protest to anyone, but because the portrayal of protest suggests that the 52% who initially wished to leave the European Union are now repentant and miraculously have become educated to the cause of the Remainers.

The long discussions in the television studios are stacked with mistruths and fear-tipped harpoons are shot from the mouths of disingenuous politicians. The top 5% of earners are going to deliver the 95% to the glorious Kingdom of Milk & Honey by paying a little extra tax – the poverty-stricken, the homeless, and all those who don't generate wealth shall inherit all the benefits society can offer including free broadband as they trudge to the food banks. Eternal riches shall shower the 95% in luxury and the nasty 5% shall suffer until their dying days.

Bombarding viewers' ears are promises that only Jeremy Corbyn and John McDonnell believe are the keys to the Great Offices of State; there seems to be no comprehension that a majority of adults do not find substance in fairytales. Simultaneously Jo Swinson and her gang of Liberal Democrats are pretending that 52% of the electorate has vanished since 2016 by promising to revoke Article 50 when they are swept to power by the miracle brooms from The Sorcerer's Apprentice. Delusion permeates from Westminster and infiltrates our living rooms via the television screen.

The young women who knocked on my door were destined to receive abuse on unwelcoming doorsteps. Those who are armed with paper swords shall see them bend when the wind blows. They were sent to the streets with an invalid purpose and economically outrageous promises that could never be financed by a small tax rise payable by the 5% of top earners. Their mission to convert the silent majority was doomed from the outset.

However, folk are at liberty to cast their votes however they choose.

REMAINERS, LEAVERS & DEMOCRATS

The days to the General Election get fewer and bitter words swirl in television studios. The pundits and the sitting members of parliament believe the vote will be won or lost on manifesto pledges or be a rerun of the 2016 Referendum. No one can be denied an opinion and between the extremes of leaving the European Union without a settlement and the Liberal Democrat's promise to revoke Article 50, there lies a mass of viewpoints that fit a mass of political ideologies. There is talk of soft and hard Brexits, the nationalization of railway and water companies, compensation for the WASPY women, 20,000 more police officers, 50,000 more nurses, the building of 40 hospitals, and a plethora of ideas that politicians may believe will sway a floating voter. A voter has a right to decide what is attractive and credible, and it must be said that a majority of parliamentarians think this is what a voter primarily considers. But unlike any previous General Election held in the United Kingdom the electorate of 2019 is split into three major factions that each boils with outrage over opposing forces.

The Remainers are entitled to hold their views even though they have been defeated in the 2016 Referendum. If they believe that being aligned with Europe for over four decades is beneficial to the United Kingdom, then that is their choice. The experiences of many warn that change is risky and fraught with uncertainty. When folk are comfortable with their present way of life it is fair to suggest that it is not sensible to alter course. For many in these islands, strong links to Europe exist and these links are reciprocated by many dwellers in continental Europe too. Never in history has there been such a close relationship between the countries of mainland Europe and the peoples of the United Kingdom. Citizens under the age of forty-five are the modern British-Europeans and they are entitled to place their loyalties wherever they wish.

And the privilege of choice is afforded to the Leavers in equal measure. Many Leavers who recall a time when our parliament was sovereign, and our destiny was the sole prerogative of both our Houses of Parliament will rue the passing of many decades of change. The older generations especially hark back to the 'good old days' when fishing fleets filled our harbors and we lived in a society that proved less multicultural. Hoards of Leavers perhaps believe sentimentally that the United Kingdom was a better place before Ted Heath signed the wicked papers that led us to the Common Market. 'We were masters of our own affairs, and answerable to no one,' they may cry. But old Leavers or young Leavers they too are entitled to their viewpoint and individually possess only one vote as do the Remainers.

But who amongst those touting for our votes championed the faction that spoke for our dying Democracy barely breathing on the green seats in the House of Commons? Democracy has been our system since Simon de Monfort set up parliament in 1265. Sure, there have been interruptions, but generally, we have survived in a democratic union for over 750 years. Democracy has served us well, and we as reasonable people have obeyed its simple rule: the losers shall accede to the will of the majority.

The will of the majority spoke clearly in the 2016 Referendum and for a brief period, Democracy remained healthy and rejuvenated the minds of 17.4 million voters. After David Cameron's resignation, the task of leaving the European Union fell into the hands of Theresa May who lost her commons' majority at the 2017 General Election. The opportunity to thwart the referendum result was seized by the Remainers. There followed over two years of battles between the weak executive and the determined legislature; parliament became an arena of disgrace which all decent democrats condemned unreservedly.

However, when Mrs. May stepped down and was succeeded by Boris Johnson both the Leavers and those who hoped that Democracy could be revived gained a champion, and for the first time since the 2016 Referendum result was announced the tide began turning in favor of the 17.4 million majority. Life was breathed into the dying body slumped on the green benches of Parliament. Those who had objectively watched

politics work for many decades surely knew then that a
Conservative majority government was on its way.
Perspicacious Remainers must have quaked in their boots
once they realized Mr. Johnson was collecting approbation
from not only those who had voted to leave the European
Union but from the reasonable voters who knew Democracy
lay in peril. It is true to say that not a single voter deserted
the cause of the Leavers because he/she believed in
democracy, yet tens or even hundreds of thousands of voters
prioritized their adherence to the democratic principle over
their desire to remain in the European family of nations.

The silent masses lay in waiting anticipating the knock-out
blow that would be delivered on December 12th. Contrary to
the scatter-brained opinions of pundits and deluded
politicians, it was clear to the objective thinker that the
combined might of Leavers and Democrats would prove
overwhelming to those who'd attempted to thwart
democracy. As days diminished an increasing number of
observers began to accept that a Conservative majority was
likely.

THE EXIT POLL

Two minutes to ten o'clock on December 12th and a thought
went out to those two young women who had battled
freezing conditions to promote the virtues of a Jeremy
Corbyn-led government. Were they sitting wine-glass in

hand awaiting a victory? Doubtless, somewhere there were deluded loyalists until just after the clock chimed ten.

The exit poll predicts a Conservative majority of 86 seats. Democracy took a huge breath and was instantly restored to life; the electorate of the United Kingdom had spoken, and this time it would not be ignored.

Two surprises came immediately after the announcement that the Labour Party had been thrashed: John McDonnell, the Shadow Chancellor, conceded defeat when it usually takes until the early hours for the losers to admit that they've lost an election, and secondly the number of folks from the world of politics who seemed shocked at the size of the predicted Conservative majority. Perhaps it was only at this moment that those who'd stymied the will of the people in the 2016 Referendum realized the monumental wave of revulsion that had built in the country during the past three years. Not only the Leavers had taken revenge on those parliamentarians who failed to uphold the people's will, but the true democrats of this nation had also backed them up and agreed with Mr. Johnson to *Get Brexit Done*. The outcome of the election said more about the mistrust the populace held for scores of MPs than it did for upholding a particular political belief. The voting public supported Mr. Johnson because he stood with the people and never deviated from the cause that Democracy must never be allowed to die.

THE RESULT

The Conservatives had been blessed with an 80 seat majority that put the party on equal standing with the governments led by both Margaret Thatcher and Tony Blair. The days of minorities were over and so too the endless defeats of the executive by the legislature. Boris Johnson now had the power to fulfill the promises in his party's manifesto and the substantial victory had destroyed the anti-democratic groans of Remainers. The Brexit argument died at the ballot box and three years of the agonizing debate was dead. And as Mr. Johnson said from his lectern in Downing Street his job now is to unite the country and reward the voters who, maybe for the first time, had placed their trust in a Conservative Administration. Jo Swinson and her Liberal Democrat party were firmly informed what the voters had thought of her idea to revoke Article 50, and Jeremy Corbyn grudgingly had to admit to himself what millions of British voters had known for years, he would never become Prime Minister because he lacked both the personality and the skills to govern one of the wealthiest nations on earth.

There should be no glory in success and no shame in defeat when the result of a General Election becomes clear. The winners should humbly accept that they have been afforded a huge responsibility and set about the tasks needed for the country to prosper during their tenure in power. And the losers should patiently and methodically set about performing their own post-mortems and not shy from the realities of how it all went wrong. Lessons learned ought to be wisdom gained, and the history of the Conservative Party over the past fifty years suggests it is more adept at conducting accurate post-mortems than the Labour Party. Since I was born in 1953 only Harold Wilson and Tony Blair have won the trust of the people for the Labour Party at a General Election. I suspect again, after the party's heaviest defeat since 1935, they again will not understand why voters rejected both their leader and their left-wing socialist policies.

One of the clues to understanding the political dynamics of the voting electorate in these islands is to imagine a rowing boat being propelled across a still lake. The oarsman sitting firmly in the center of the boat is none other than Joe Bloggs, the sole representative of the British public. To secure his passage to the other end of the lake Joe Bloggs will try not to shuffle on his seat or sway too much to the left or the right; should he do so, he will topple over and perhaps be drowned. Joe Bloggs, as with a majority of the people he represents is a centralist. All the elected prime ministers of the past sixty years have been centralists, some leaning slightly to the left and others leaning slightly to the right, but none has promoted the extreme political views that are anathema to the British voting public.

Policies that lurch to the outer wings of political thinking will always be rejected. Militarization and a compassionless society are right-wing policies that the public will never tolerate. The extreme punishment of ridiculously high taxation for those who have gained wealth and the rewarding of those who are leeches on our society are left-wing policies that will never gain traction. Governments that

neglect the law-abiding majority will always fail.
Governments that allow too much power to filter to other
organizations will fail too. There should be no hate in
politics, no jealousy, no support for minorities to raise them
above the height of the majority. A Government's primary
aim should be to create societal conditions in which the
beggar and the entrepreneur can thrive. A Government must
be fair and accept that all citizens are not equal yet afford to
all citizens the opportunities to rise beyond their present
stations. If a politician of any party espouses policies that
aim to ameliorate the lives of the many with no
overwhelming burden on the rich and no gross neglect of the
poor, then he/she will gain popularity and reap respect from
all corners of society. Contrary to the rigid belief in most
politicians that policies are everything and personalities
count for little, the opposite is true. Centralist policies will
ensure that a British politician does not exclude
himself/herself from rising to power, but even politicians
who walk a line down the very middle are far from
guaranteed to gain political success. The number one clue to
steer a party to Downing Street, that has not been heeded by
any politician (I know of) lies in the distant past. It seems to
me now, as it has done for 55 years, that politicians can't see
the wood for the trees.

THROUGH A CHILD'S EYES

In the late 1950s and early 1960s television sets were
flooding into homes of the electorate. After World War II the

western democracies were socially progressing at a rate
never before seen in history. The early rock & roll stars were
energizing youth and preparing post-war children for the
revolution that was to come in the 1960s. The children who
'should be seen and not heard' were beginning to imbibe
information from sources other than their forefathers, and so
too were their parents. A new and exciting invention quickly
became the focal point in every household and by the 1964
General Election, the voting public and those who would
someday attain voting age were seeing and hearing their
potential political masters on the glass screen in the corner
of their living rooms.

In 1963, as a ten-year-old, I'd seen John F. Kennedy
assassinated in Dallas, Texas, and was unable to understand
the reasons why a handsome young man had been shot
dead. From adult reactions to the killing, I understood that a
tragedy had occurred: Kennedy had been adored by millions,
and millions grieved his passing. So, when less than a year
later the British public were offered the choice between an
unattractive posh-spoken not-one-of-us Alec Douglas-Home
and the much younger charming man-of-the-people smiling
Yorkshireman Harold Wilson the eleven-year-old child that
was me decided that the result of the election was a
foregone conclusion: 100% Harold Wilson.

Wilson scraped home, and I'd picked a winner. Of course, in
those days children were naïve and innocent, but I felt then
that the outcome of the election was obvious: Harold Wilson
seemed a lovely guy and Alec Douglas-Home seemed aloof.
And in 1966 I picked the winner again when Wilson increased
his party's majority over the Conservative-led opposition of

Ted Heath. I'd tell my parents that voters choose the most likable face on offer.

IT GETS COMPLICATED

Retrospectively, the most difficult elections to call were those in 1970 and the two in 1974. Leaving childhood behind and witnessing industrial relations worsen, and the rising power of Trades' Unions during the late sixties had me thinking that my 'likable personality theory' was flawed. Ted Heath didn't appeal as a friendly guy and his haughty manner just didn't seem conducive to working-class voters. Now seventeen, I began to amend my thinking and accepted that a good personality may carry individuals to Downing Street, but it doesn't necessarily keep them there. I plumped for Heath, and Heath won.

But Heath's misfortune was to preside over the government that oversaw power cuts and persistently looked weak in its battles with Trades' Unions. By 1974 the electorate was faced with a choice of two men who had no good ideas of how to manage the country as inflations spiraled and strikes began to affect the lives of millions. Wilson won two General Elections, but the reality seemed to me that the country desperately needed a messiah. And when Wilson retired due to ill-health in 1976 and James Callaghan took up residence in Downing Street it didn't appear that our wait was over. The country plummeted to its lowest point and by 1979 there were heaps of rubbish on the streets of London and unburied bodies in Liverpool. Chaos reigned. The messiah landed in the form of Margaret Thatcher. To me, as an increasingly interested politically-minded observer now in his mid-twenties, there could only be one winner of the 1979 General Election.

However, the complication of my 'Pick a Prime Minister Plan' deepens; Mrs. Thatcher was a woman and she wasn't exactly charming. Thatcher had in abundance the qualities of leadership, strength, and vision. She knew where she wished to steer this country and she had the determination to get her way. Her politics of Individualism was the philosophy needed to lift our ailing nation by its bootstrings and restore its position in the world to one of respect. Oh sure, there were millions who despised Thatcher, and millions breathing today who wince when they hear her name, but without her transformation of the grim realities pervading in 1979, this country would have been bankrupt eternally. She restored Britain's position in the world and must surely be regarded as our boldest and brightest leader. The Labour Party's response to challenge her dominance came dressed as Michael Foot and Neil Kinnock. Neither Foot nor Kinnock ever had a chance of unseating her; they didn't look or behave like Prime Ministers and their policies were too reminiscent of those which led us to the catastrophe of 1979.

Thatcher reigned supreme until her followers did to her what Brutus did to Caesar. The Tories replaced her with John Major, the political gray man, and it was now that Labour should have seized the opportunity to gain political power. Before the 1992 General Election was called the Labour Party should have acknowledged that Neil Kinnock wasn't a vote winner and replaced him with a more suitable candidate to be Prime Minister. Had John Smith been at the helm of the 1992 campaign the outcome may have been different. Instead, in poverty as a single parent, I placed my total wealth of £6 at 16-1 for John Major to gain an overall majority, not because Major was a vote winner, but because Kinnock was a vote loser and would not win in twenty General Elections.

Major became Prime Minister, Kinnock resigned, then sadly John Smith who succeeded Kinnock, died prematurely in 1994. Only now, over 30 years after the Labour Party's last sensible act of exalting Harold Wilson, did it find a leader capable of winning power. The ever-smiling, handsome, genial, wanting to be liked Tony Blair took the helm of the long-sinking Labour Party Ship, and from the moment of his installation as the leader, it became clear he would sweep to power at the next General Election. His charm and enthusiasm appealed to women, his simple message of 'Like me, I'm a nice guy' appealed to millions of other voters including many Tories who had not forgiven the treacherous act of stabbing Margaret Thatcher in the back when away in Europe.

The 1997 General Election was perhaps the easiest of all results to predict: Tony Blair thrashed John Major and brought about the first Labour Administration in 18 years. It would take a miracle to wrest power away from a Blair Government providing he stuck to center-ground policies and kept on smiling.

The Conservative party faced its greatest adversary and possibly the most successful Labour Politician in history. Despite challenges by William Hague (a highly commendable Thatcherite who would have been an excellent PM), Iain Duncan Smith and Michael Howard, Blair won victories in three successive General elections until he stepped down in favor of Gordon Brown in 2007. If Major had been the Conservative gray man, then now it was Labour's turn: Brown was a dull character, unappealing to voters and was largely responsible for the poor state of the country's finances due to his long tenure as Chancellor. He remains one more example of a Labour Leader with very little hope of winning a General Election.

In 2010 I predicted a large majority for the fresh and amenable David Cameron who'd been the leader of the opposition since 2005. Cameron's mastery of parliamentary debate proved impressive and he seemed a certain winner of the General Election. However, the Liberal vote under Nick Clegg held up and Cameron failed to win an overall majority. A coalition administration was formed and Clegg, another young charmer, became Deputy Prime Minister. But Cameron got his majority in 2015 when he defeated Ed Miliband's Labour Party and the Liberal vote collapse disastrously. For many observers it looked like Cameron was in for a long stay in Downing Street; he stood in his late forties with a bright future ahead.

In my opinion, it wasn't Cameron's decision to call a referendum in 2016 that led to his downfall, but his decision to tell the electorate which way they should vote. It seems insane to me that if a leader cedes power to those beneath him, if only temporarily to secure their opinion, then the leader should abstain on a pre-vote judgment and promise to deliver the will delivered from the referendum with his full support. No leader can ask the electorate to decide the United Kingdom's course then tell the voters that they are wrong if they do not agree with him: he did the honorable thing by resigning but his departure was brought about by his own ill-judgment of taking sides.

We are close to the present. The reliable, capable Mrs. May didn't need to sparkle in 2017 to defeat the impossible to elect Jeremy Corbyn. Had she not bungled her campaign by constantly referring to 'I' and 'Me' and 'My' instead of 'We', 'Us' and 'the Conservative Party' she would surely have achieved a similar electoral result as Boris Johnson. It is now all grist to the mill; the history lesson is over, and I shall make my case on how to win a General Election.

WINNERS LEARN FROM WINNERS

As previously stated, no candidate for the office of prime minister should harbor views that deviate too far from the center ground of British politics. If they do, they are doomed to failure and shall be rejected by the electorate.

Without a doubt, the political views of Jeremy Corbyn were the most extreme ever promoted in this country in modern history and whether or not he possessed the character, the looks, or the charm to be a tenant of Downing Street his policies and his left-wing status prohibited him from doing so. The Labour Party made a grave error of judgment in ever believing he would lead it to power.

The most obvious winners in British political history (1960-2020) have been Margaret Thatcher, Tony Blair, and Harold Wilson; while Thatcher possessed unerring common sense, great leadership and vision, the two male Prime Ministers were enormously attractive individuals whose charm enticed the electorate to vote for the Labour Party.

All male prime ministers elected to office during this period fit into the age group of 40 to 60 years. All male prime ministers elected to office were attractive personalities that were not averse to smiling.

Two female prime ministers elected to office during this period fit into the age group of 40 to 60 years. Both female prime ministers elected to office were solid characters, politically skilled and who showed devotion to duty and a motherly affection toward the peoples of this country.

No elected prime minister has been bald, too old, too young, had glaring physical defects, had speech impediments, had a broad accent, had obvious peculiarities, had known bad habits, was ugly or rude or aggressive or ignorant. No prime minister has shown envy of the rich or disdain for the poor. Among their virtues were charm, intelligence, foresight, understanding, sociability, compassion, respectability, trustworthiness, honesty and unflappability.

In general, the prospect of becoming Prime Minister if half the electorate finds the candidate unlikable is dismal. A prerequisite to attaining the highest office is to own a character akin to a voter's favorite neighbor: if a voter wouldn't want the candidate living next door, then he/she wouldn't want the candidate in Downing Street. (Only Ted Heath defies this rule).

My ranking of prime ministers based solely on their chances of winning a General Election are out of ten:

MARGARET THATCHER 10, TONY BLAIR 10, HAROLD WILSON 8, BORIS JOHNSON 7+, DAVID CAMERON 7, THERESA MAY 5, EDWARD HEATH 4, JOHN MAJOR 4, GORDON BROWN 3, JAMES CALLAGHAN 3.

My ranking of party leaders based solely on their chances of winning a General Election are out of ten:

WILLIAM HAGUE 5, JOHN SMITH 5, IAIN DUNCAN SMITH 3, MICHAEL HOWARD 3, ALEC DOUGLAS-HOME 3, NEIL KINNOCK 2, ED MILIBAND 2, MICHAEL FOOT 1, JEREMY CORBYN 1.

IT'S PUBLIC PERCEPTION THAT COUNTS

No matter how amicable, generous, loveable or friendly the candidates for the Office of Prime Minister are in private it is the perception the public has of them that gives them a chance of success. I do not wish to disparage any of the contenders; they are all fine people for devoting great portions of their life to public service. But since the advent of television, for it is primarily through tv appearances that candidates reveal their characteristics to the masses, how they come over on the small screen is a matter of unequaled gravity.

When Harold Wilson appeared on screen with The Beatles, he must have gained thousands of hitherto skeptical voters. When Margaret Thatcher ignored the advice of US President Reagan and ordered the British troops to retake the Falkland Isles she was perceived as a great British champion. Blair showed his youthful prowess by kicking a ball in the air. Johnson was never afraid of clowning or exposing his human frailties. Cameron talked about his ill-fated son and revealed the joys and sorrows of parenthood. Even May's ordinary love of walking gained admirers. We saw Ted Heath in his yacht, heard Major disclose that his father performed in a circus and many other endearing snippets that built a public perception of those who became Prime Minister. But several of the also-rans leave no endearing memories and the perceptions of them owned by the electorate may have suffered as a consequence.

It is simply not enough to speak of policies and to criticize the policies of opposition parties. The electorate is more susceptible to placing crosses on ballot papers against the names of those they admire as humans than they are to vote for a pleasing policy. We agree with lots of strangers' opinions; it doesn't follow that we wish to allow them to invade our television screens for the next five years or place our hopes for a prosperous future in their hands. We must be content, for a while at least, to live with the candidate we promote to power. And collectively, perception is the bus that carries the victor to Downing Street.

And to some extent, the perception the public has of those MPs who support a candidate for the highest office matters too. During the last parliament before Boris Johnson was given an overwhelming endorsement of the public confidence in his ability to move the country to fresh pastures, there were scenes in the House of Commons unlike any witnessed in the past sixty years. Vitriolic speeches, malicious accusations, labels of liar and untrustworthiness poured primarily from MPs on the opposition benches. Faces of MPs actually contorted with hate, teeth got bared in an aggressive manner, and arms flailed wildly, and fingers wagged like threatening knives. These uncivilized behaviors were viewed by millions of voters watching the action on television and did nothing to endear people to the Parties that were guilty of allowing such displays.

Hate, jealousy, vilification, and abuse will swiftly deliver MPs to the exit door of politics and respect, civility and generosity of sentiment will keep an MP fastened to the green benches. Those who seek power must be above hateful attacks and stick to the moderate language of disagreement; there is a distinct difference between a strong leader's oratory and the vile used by a street thug, and those presently vying for leadership of the Labour Party should be mindful of the tone that they adopt.

TWO LONG-HELD THOUGHTS

Show a four-year-old child, pairs of photographs of the primary contenders in General Elections from 1964-2019 and ask the child to pick the winner. I suspect the child will select as many winners as the most astute political commentators and certainly be more successful than the average political activist. What does this tell us?

And secondly, since the age of Michael Foot, I have often dreamed of encouraging the Labour Party to discover a Paul Newman lookalike actor and training him to be a politician. The handsome actor needs to learn responses, utterly suitable soundbites in the style of Tony Blair, smile profusely and pose for photographs with ordinary citizens. I am certain that if our actor performed to the best of his abilities the likelihood of him becoming Prime Minister would be far greater than many others who have challenged for the key to Number Ten. What does this tell us?

Appearance and public perception are almost everything. If a party leader can't pass the four-year-old test or doesn't possess charm, good looks or some other outstanding quality, then that party leader has barely a hope of winning a majority in parliament.

A RECAP OF SUCCESS

Let us briefly collate the reasons why individuals became
Prime Ministers and reveal the clues that enable such
observers as me to predict the outcome of General Elections.
It is not supremely difficult to work out what the electorate
thinks of candidates as the critical voting day nears.

Harold Wilson was blessed with the common touch and knew
precisely the persona to adopt to gain public approbation.
He came over as smart, intelligent, friendly, and a man of the
people for the people.

Edward Heath was fortunate in so much as Wilson's sparkle
dimmed and that the public was willing to trust another
leader to manage a country in stagnation.

Wilson won again because the country judged the power cuts
as intolerable.

When Margaret Thatcher succeeded James Callaghan (an
unelected PM) the country had sunk to its lowest point in
modern history.

Thatcher defeated both Michael Foot and Neil Kinnock
because she had vision and leadership greater than any other
leader in modern history.

John Major won his election because the alternative of Neil
Kinnock was so unappealing.

The fresh young face of Tony Blair with his call of New Labour
enticed millions of voters to commence a new era much

distinguishable from Thatcherism. He remained in power because the country seemed stable and the Tories couldn't fracture his popularity.

David Cameron and Nick Clegg too were bright and attractive compared to Gordon Brown who presided over a dying Labour Government and a failing economy, and it was only Cameron's later mistake of not remaining impartial in the 2016 Referendum that brought his premiership to a close.

Theresa May acceded the leadership, and she may have stayed there for years if her 2017 electoral campaign hadn't been so ill-managed.

And finally, when Boris Johnson took the side of the people against the obstructive parliamentarians, he was assured of a resounding victory in the 2019 General Election. He has the potential to be a very notable Prime Minister providing he governs sensibly and fulfills the promises of his party's manifesto.

LABOUR'S HOPE OF RECOVERY

In the short term, the appeal of the Labour Party depends solely on whether the party learns the lessons embedded in its history. After Michael Foot's disastrous tenure (1980-1983) the party did not recognize the importance of having an attractive figurehead and replaced Foot with Kinnock who was barely much of an improvement. The party clung to left-wing policies and gave Thatcher an easy passage through the 1980s.

Now, with 2020 merely days away, the party seems determined to elect a female leader with the bizarre idea that it's time it had one - a pathetic, irrational judgment that again will worsen the situation after Corbyn leaves his post. Those with any sense will call for the most appropriate candidate to be elected, be the candidate male or female.

If the Labour Party does not desert its left-wing policies it not only faces at least another decade out of office, it faces oblivion and the threat of another party's formation. Merely changing Corbyn for a blunt-speaking northern female will not alter fortune one iota.

A period of calm reflection is needed. Sensible voices must amplify the fact that the party's greatest successes were gained by Blair and all the party members must ask themselves why Blair was so dominant and such as Foot, Kinnock, and Corbyn were so pitifully inept.

As an outsider, I see a modicum of merit in Stephen Kinnock and far greater merit in Andy Burnham, the current Mayor of Manchester. Both men are inoffensive and speak with reasonableness and without the use of inflammatory phrases. They are steady politicians who are capable of stabilizing Labour's turbulent recent past. But it will be a miracle if anyone in the next five years manages to hold a candle to Boris Johnson's ebullient and rising star. Labour's best hope is to find a genial character, camp for years in the left-center of British politics, be gracious losers, and hope in perhaps ten years hence Johnson's star will have dimmed, or his successor will be a grim substitute. If the Labour Party repeats historical mistakes, then Tony Blair's name may well stand forever as the last on its small list of successful candidates for the Office of Prime Minister.

LEEDS, MAY 2021

Few things are certain in British Politics but we can generally expect sitting governments to lose many seats in council elections, often hundreds of seats, and we can expect governments who've had lengthy stays of power to lose bi-elections. And when a government has suffered allegations of sleaze, as the present one had done in the last part of 2020 and the first part of 2021, doom is usually the outcome. Those observers of the multitude of elections in early May 2021 will have noticed that the reliable patterns of the past did not extend to the contest between Johnson's Conservative and Sir Keir Starmer's supposedly rejuvenated Labour Party.

As advocated in previous pages, Labour never learns from past mistakes.

I have spoken about the importance of a charismatic party leader and reiterated many times that political policies always play second fiddle to personalities in the public conscience. To many voters the terms center-left or middle-ground are meaningless and incomprehensible; they care far less about what a party political leader says but for more about how he or she says it. Millions of voters not particularly excited by policy detail can be allured by a genial smiling face or an appealing character whose faults are forgivable. Politicians of all persuasions simply do not accept this undeniable truth and they become serial losers due to their refusal to acknowledge its validity.

To explain why the present Labour Party has made little or no progress since they finally abandoned Jeremy Corbyn in the Spring of 2020 is remarkably simple. My advice was ignored – it chose to overlook probably the only candidate who is capable of increasing a share of the public vote, Andy Burnham. The Labour Party ousted Jeremy Corbyn and replaced him with the extra-bland Sir Keir Starmer who seems to be a steady ship without a propellor. I do not doubt that Sir Keir Starmer is a decent, inoffensive man with a good intellect but he is unlikely to win a Personality of the Year Award. He is even less charming than dull John Major and exceedingly unlikely to stir former Labour loyalists from the comfort of their armchairs to the voting booths.

Boris Johnson may be prone to gaffs and overseeing dubious acts by those connected to his administration but any wounds inflicted by the wolves of the media will swiftly heal when the public momentarily glances at the alternative and realizes that the devil you know is preferable to watching paint dry at the dispatch box in the House of Commons. Contrary to Labour crying that Johnson had the success of the vaccine program on his side, this was not the reason the opposition party made no progress on its snail-pace march to power.

In the past sixty years, Labour has been led by only two charismatic figures, namely Harold Wilson and Tony Blair – they both won three General Elections: other Labour leaders in this period won none!

THE COMING YEARS

It is impossible to envisage calm waters flowing throughout the remainder of Boris Johnson's premiership; coupled with his star quality is his propensity to make blunders. Johnson is destined to be a leader renowned for successes and memorable for mistakes that could have been averted. He will likely stay in office until his parliamentary colleagues see his attraction wane. The Conservative Party is skilled in determining when a leader's popularity is diving and is ruthlessly willing to act in such circumstances.

But for opposition parties, it is not enough to hope that a sitting Prime Minister will show sufficient incompetence to hand the key to Downing Street to the Leader of the Opposition. The voting public will always side with a suspect Prime Minster rather than elect to office an unremarkable replacement. An alternative Prime Minister must have something new and refreshing to offer the nation, especially characteristics that are endearing.

The coming years, unless a catastrophe of majestic proportions besets this incumbent government, seem safely in the keep of the Conservative Party. No amount of policy shifts or re-shuffles of Sir Keir Starmer's shadow cabinet are capable of widespread changes of public opinion. The Labour Party's legacy of forever 'picking the wrong man' will keep it in opposition for years to come.

As far as I can see into the future the aforementioned catastrophe is Starmer's single hope of power. He does not possess the qualities of a political winner and is very likely to join the list of also-rans after the 2024 (?) General Election. By then, Conservative rule will extend to 14 years and Labour's chiefs will still be squabbling over policy decisions.

As previously stated, Labour's single hope of reversing the trend of voter desertion lies with the choice of promoting Andy Burnham to leadership. Of course, presently he is not a sitting member of parliament, but this obstacle is not insurmountable.

Burnham's popularity as a politician – a Labour politician - can be compared with Blair, Wilson, Shirley Williams and Harriet Harman; few other Labour front or backbenchers can be listed as widely likable at some point or another during their political careers.

In 2017 Burnham was elected as Mayor of Manchester and was re-elected with a greater vote-share and a larger number of voters in 2021. This second victory came in the face of the continuing rejection of a Labour Party in turmoil and at a time when Sir Keir Starmer was pushing forward his 'New Leadership' message.

It appears to me, that not inviting Andy Burnham to accept the challenge of resurrecting his party's fortunes is insane.

He is the one person who can be guaranteed to increase its vote-share in any future election. He is the one person who can stop the rot before the Labour Party plunges into oblivion. And I am not implying that Burnham can miraculously sweep his party to power but simply promulgating my theory that voters are attracted to personalities rather than policies. Burnham has what both Wilson and Blair possessed, star quality, and if the Labour Party continues to overlook its single path to progress then future updates to this book may be discussing the possibility of how and when the Green Party can seize power.

See the following advertisements:

(ADVERTISEMENTS)

Ken Ross novels including his recent romantic/erotic suspense series of:

WASTED PAIN
https://www.amazon.com/gp/product/B07NSFSJJ5/ref=db s_a_def_rwt_bibl_vppi_i1

The opening story where a homeless gal is found freezing in an alley by an older guy. He takes her to his house and cares for her. The gal won't tell him anything of her past and won't even tell him her name. She comes and goes, but gradually a relationship develops, and it gets increasingly hotter. He wants the gal to stay forever, but neither of them knows where they're heading. He loses her, finds her, the story twists and turns and the suspense builds to a crescendo. Will disaster strike, or will they find happiness together?

PROTECTION: sex, revenge & romance

https://www.amazon.com/gp/product/B07NKFQN3F/ref=d bs_a_def_rwt_bibl_vppi_i5

The characters return during this story but its central theme is the relationship between the older guy's son, Jerry, and his three gals who are sisters. They are hot from the beginning and it seems to be a tale wholly about sex, but then the shocks start to arrive. They are pulled emotionally to places they don't want to go. Their lives fluctuate between ecstasy and despair, and again the suspense increases throughout. Happiness or sadness? Hey, read and discover the ending.

BODIES

https://www.amazon.com/gp/product/B07QYGXWTB/ref= dbs_a_def_rwt_bibl_vppi_i6

 The third book of this series and probably the most shocking of the stories. Jerry and his gals have a new addition and are continuing their adventure until he betrays them. A disaster turns into an even greater tragedy and their world starts to crumble. Does the story give any of them happiness in the end, or do they face a total collapse of everything they've previously known?

MAMA

https://www.amazon.com/gp/product/B07VKDK2CC/ref=d bs_a_def_rwt_bibl_vppi_i5

The fourth book in the series sees Jerry, Patsy and Erica return to Crickenville where they come across an unexpected visitor at the gals' Pa's shack. Mama is a character from the past and she has secrets that aren't easy to discover. Once more the adventurous trio meets danger as they go on a rescue mission to save a couple of teenage gals held prisoners by Mama's uncles. But more is to come including the greatest shock of Patsy's life.

BROKEN SISTERS – the fifth novel that deals with the aftermath of Mama's disclosure about Erica's birth. Jerry needs to work miracles to keep his group together as the strained relationship between his favorite gals threatens to blow them apart. They return to Crickenville to unearth more long-hidden truths, and one truth in particular has great significance.

GOODBYE VIOLET The sixth novel of the series reunites Jerry, Patsy & Erica with the twins as once more they go to Crickenville. There is bloodshed, uncertainty, and it looks like they'll have to get out of America to retain their freedom. As usual, the sex is endless and fulfilling but this time their crimes are the worst they've ever committed.

REVIEWS ON AMAZON ARE MUCH APPRECIATED.

Other novels include:

A CROSS OF CROCUSES

https://www.amazon.com/gp/product/B07KWFHN1G/ref= dbs_a_def_rwt_bibl_vppi_i0

An English-style novel dealing with aspects of aging and how two old folk in their ninth decade of life cope when problems of daily existence arrive. They have five children, but can they depend on them, and which of the children will be helpful? The ones who come forward are not those they thought would do so. This heartbreaking story awaits us all, whether as an aging parent or with aging parents of your own. And it is surprising what happens to folk when they are under pressure. An amazing tale with outstanding reviews.

ANN – irresistible spirit

https://www.amazon.com/gp/product/B07JYJNV3C/ref=db s_a_def_rwt_bibl_vppi_i4

Another English story of teenage romance begins in 1960s Leeds on the backstreets. It's a beautiful tale following the two protagonists through a fifty-year relationship. Recounted by the man, there's detail of how love blossoms, how sex is learned, a marriage of youngsters and early parenthood. But then she makes a terrible mistake when they've got a houseful of children, and they separate. But their bond is unbreakable, and it endures a lifetime and ultimately meets tragedy. A very moving story of love.

THE LADS WILL HAVE BLOOD

https://www.amazon.com/gp/product/B015PSW48M/ref= dbs_a_def_rwt_bibl_vppi_i7

A crime thriller about a father and a gang of estate lads who have seen James Cornleak face a corrupt trial and receive an eighteen-year prison sentence because of bent evidence. They are determined to get even with the police, and with the justice system, but both authorities are more corrupt than they ever thought, and retribution isn't easy. This fast-moving tale takes you through social unrest, murder, and a pile of mysteries. Can the father of James Cornleak and his friends ever get even with authority? Maybe they can, but it's difficult to guess how they do it.

AN OLD AFFAIR

https://www.amazon.com/gp/product/B07SWRHGKS/ref=dbs_a_def_rwt_bibl_vppi_i1

A romance for single older readers who have thought about giving up their independence and finding a new love later in life. When Harry Morgan goes chasing an old flame, he discovers that renewing an old affair comes with complications.

ROSALEE'S PUNISHMENT

https://www.amazon.com/gp/product/B082H56FBW/ref=dbs_a_def_rwt_bibl_vppi_i7

Mike begins a letter to his long-time lover who has recently died in an automobile accident, but it quickly becomes a narrative of how he survives without her. From mourning, he descends into depravity and wonders why his lover's best friend is so interested in him. A shocking tale of sexual desire.

ANY REVIEWS ON AMAZON, OR GOODREADS, ARE MUCH APPRECIATED.